Twenty Months in Southland, 1867-69.

An early account of Southland's people, settlements, and landscape.

By 'A. Tasmanian'

Twenty Months in Southland 1867-69.

Acknowledgements: Thanks to the wonderful libraries and museums of Southland, in particular the Southland Museum & Art Gallery. Map sections courtesy of the Australian National Library. Thanks to Lloyd Esler for the feedback, comments and advice.

Dornie Publishing Company
Grasmere, Invercargill
www.dorniepublishing.tk

Original text © 'A. Tasmanian' and The Mercury (Hobart)
2012 Edition © Dornie Publishing
Images © named individuals or institutions.
All rights reserved.
Second edition Jan. 2012.
First edition Nov. 2010
ISBN 978-0-473-18025-6
Cover design by Strawberrymouse Designs

Twenty Months in Southland 1867-69.

"New Zealand was colonised initially by those Australians who had the initiative to escape."

Robert Muldoon (NZ Prime Minister), 1981

Twenty Months in Southland 1867-69.

Twenty Months in Southland 1867-69.

Introduction

This booklet contains the reminiscences and observations of an adventurous Tasmanian during his travels around Southland and South Otago in the late 1860s. The anonymous narrator, using the pseudonym 'A. Tasmanian', articulately describes a number of the local characters, settlements and economic prospects of early Southland. He discusses aspects of natural history encountered in the region such as: native plants, animals, landscape and weather. In the last three chapters the author gives an account of working on a sheep station and a vivid portrayal of the methods (and frustrations) of goldmining in southern New Zealand. After a 20 month sojourn from 1867-69 the narrator returns back to Tasmania to tell his tale.

This account was originally published in sections from Wednesday 1st December 1869 to Friday 18th March 1870 in *The Mercury* (Hobart). In order to provide an historical setting and make some of the language more accessible to modern readers there are some brief footnotes. Other than these small inclusions the account is unchanged.

Twenty Months in Southland 1867-69.

Contents

Chapter I

The Voyage	9
The Bluff Special Train	10
Bog and Bush	11
Mappo, Manuka, Totara, Pines, Supple-Jack, "Lawyer"- Tutu	11

Chapter II

The Oreti River	15
Invercargill, Pavement, Water, Shops, "The Company"	15
Hotels	17
Wagons, Eastern Road	17
Cockatooers, Company's Produce	18

Chapter III

The Mataura, Dangerous Fords	21
Suspension Bridge, Lampreys	22
Hokanui, Tutu, "Blue-bottle Flies"	22
Waimea, "Wild Irishman", "Paradise Duck"	23
"Another Providence", Switzers, Tapanui, Lignite	25

Chapter IV

Saw Mills of Tapanui, Billiards	27
Fatality of Tutu, Mr. Pinkerton's Station	28
Waimea, Long Ridge	29
Grand View	30

Chapter V

The Elbow	31
"Devil's Stair-case", Lake Wakatip Gold-diggings	32
New River Flat, "Billy-goat Park", Moonlight Range	33
Family Bog, Mr. Basstian's Station	35
The Aparima - Longwood Range	35

Chapter VI

Cross the Otautau, Mrs. McCoy	39
Riverton, Jacob's River	40
Maori Kaik	41
Moleskins versus Mabs	42
Mutton Birding, Fish	42
War-Dance	43

Chapter VII
    Station Life , Snow, Mountain Rifts 45
    "Spaniards" 46
    Eel-fishing, Mosquitoes 47
    Shearing and Shearers 48
    Howraki 49
    Wool-carting, "Futur", Rats, Seagulls, Wind 50
    Sheen smothered, Billets 52

Chapter VII
    Prospecting for Gold, First Camp 55
    Track Cutting and Cradling, Snow and Ice Flooded Out ... 56
    Try Again, Wood-hens & their Antics 57
    How we Caught and Cooked Them, Swallows, Crane 58

Chapter IX
    Prospecting Again, Cutting a Face 61
    Building Dam and Hut 61
    Blue Ducks, Hawks 63

Chapter X
    Gold Failing, Remove, Flooded Out again, Building Hut ... 65
    Making Dams, Kokabulla, Welsh and French 66
    Cau-cau, Kakapo 68
    "Charleys", Recall 68

Further reading 71

Twenty Months in Southland 1867-69.

Chapter I

The Voyage - The Bluff Special Train - Bog and Bush Mappo – Manuka – Totara – Pines - Supple-Jack – "Lawyer" - Tutu.

Since my recent return from New Zealand, after nearly two years' sojourn, I have been so sharply catechized[1] as to where I went, what I saw, what I did, and what I thought of it, that it appears to me the best plan is to answer everybody by narrating my experiences, as briefly as fidelity will admit. I travelled nearly all over Southland, and will first make an epitome of my wanderings, so as to give a general topographical outline of the province; and supply details of practical work-a-day life, afterwards.

Of my voyage thither from Melbourne little need be said; and that is fortunate, for right little could I say. Prostrated in body and mind by the most horrible and least commiserated of temporary maladies[2], all, save suffering, was a blank for some days. As a follow sufferer on another voyage pithily put it:- "*First I was afraid I was going to die, and then I was afraid I wasn't.*"

The earliest symptom of returning animation I well remember. I was aroused to a puzzled feeling of envious admiration of the stewardess's skill in legerdemain[3] - if that be the correct term. The ship was rolling, pitching, and otherwise demeaning herself in most uneasy fashion, and landsmen infirm of footing, were holding on with desperate grip, to any friendly projection in their neighbourhood, when I beheld the stewardess aforesaid, ascend the companion, steady, serene, and smiling, bearing in one hand a plate heaped up with bread and butter, and in the other five cups of coffee, piled into a column, the second saucer covering the first cup,

---
[1] Thoroughly questioned or interrogated
[2] Sea-sickness
[3] Sleight of hand

and so on to the summit. With charmed gaze I watched her tripping lightly to and fro, without a flaw in her course, setting down her plate, and handing off a brimming cup from the pile, till all were distributed; and I dreamily thought that some day I would try to do the like on shore, but never have. I think that stewardess would excel the Japanese themselves, if she liked to devote her remarkable talent to top-spinning, or bamboo-walking.

Invercargill being my destination, I quitted the steamer[4] at the Bluff, where vessels coming to Invercargill now land their cargoes and passengers. It is a head-land of some 900 feet in height, at the foot of which lies the small village known by the same name. There is nothing grand or picturesque in the scene; the hill slopes gradually backward and upward, covered with low scrub and New Zealand flax (*Phormium tenax*). A small wharf has been erected, of limber, which only affords space for two vessels to lie alongside at one time. The little settlement consists of three public houses and about twenty people, so that the arrival of vessels with many passengers, occasions an extraordinary sensation. At the time when the great rush to the Lake Wakatip[5] diggings took place, the population was considerably larger, but many buildings are at present empty, as the traffic to Wakatip is now carried on by way of Dunedin.

On going to the railway station to take my passage to Invercargill, I found that if eight passengers could be found who would take return tickets, a special train would run immediately, so as to be back, whilst the steamer waited for the mails. That number being ready, we started, in a second-class carriage, fare 5s. single ticket. No first class carriages are laid on, and only one trip each day usually made[6]. The pace is about fifteen miles an hour, and the distance 20 miles. In one particular this railway is peculiarly accommodating, for if a passenger hails the train at any part of the road, the engine-driver at

---

[4] The main steamers doing the Melbourne-Bluff direct journey in 1867 were the *Tararua, Alhambra, Rangitoto* and *Omeo*.
[5] (*sic*) Wakatipu. The Central Otago gold-rush began in 1862.
[6] The Bluff – Invercargill railway opened only a matter of months before our narrator arrived in 1867.

once slackens the not too impetuous speed, and pulls up like an old stage coachman, to pick up the fare.

The country we traversed is an alternation of bog and bush; over the long low tracts of bog, embankments are made, to receive the sleepers and rails; and two intermediate "platforms" occur between the Bluff and Invercargill[7].

The timber seemed to my Tasmanian eyes, accustomed to our giant eucalyptuses very small, it being a rarity to see a tree three feet through. The tops are nearly all blown off by the perpetual winds, and remind one of dismasted ships, as they raise their shattered stumps above the under-scrub. This in many parts consists of Mappo and Manuka, interlaced thickly with an almost impenetrable network of crooning plants, here known as "vines". Mappo[8] is a very pretty shrub, not unlike the Tasmanian *Noteloa*, but with fruit more resembling a *pittosporum*, the green husk opening when ripe and showing the cluster of claret-coloured seeds within, covered with a gummy kind of moisture. Manuka is the Maori name for the tea-tree (*Leptospermum*) which is identical I believe, with that of Tasmania.

The trees in this part are chiefly pines. The Totara[9] wears the brightest green of all, and is conspicuous at a distance, from its light yellowish tint. The stems are bare till near the top, and that is ragged-looking and blown to one side by the prevalent N.W. winds. The black, red, and white pines look, to a stranger very much alike, just as our gum trees do; but when known better are very distinct. The black-pine[10] has dark wood, a dark, hard, scaly bark, dark green foliage, and a small red berry, which is eaten by birds. The white pine[11] is so nailed from the wood, which is a light, soft deal; in other respects the tree very much resembles the black pine.

---

[7] The great swamp was gradually drained and is now known as Seaward Moss. Early road building attempts failed as the swamp swallowed up the roading material (See Hall-Jones 1976, p.59-69).
[8] (*sic*) Mapou, - *Myrsine australis*.
[9] Totara - *Podocarpus totara*
[10] Matai - *Podocarpus spicatus*
[11] Kahikatea - *Podocarpus dacrydioides*

The red pine[12] is a larger tree than either of the former, indeed one of the largest trees in Southland; its foliage is like that of the Norfolk Island pine, (*Arancaria excelsa*) but more leafy, and the long shoots of a young tree droop very gracefully, but as the tree grows older, they become shorter and stiffer. The wood has a reddish tinge, hence its name.

Of the "vines" which inter-twist and tie the shrubs, trees, and themselves together in one inextricable labyrinth, there are many varieties. The one named "supple-jack" has jointed stems like bamboo, as thick as one's finger. The clematis[13], with its fragrant wealth of lovely white starry blossoms, is apparently but a larger variety of the kind so common in Tasmania and Victoria, and looked like the face of an old friend, amidst the many new forms which surrounded me in this dreary wilderness of bush and bog. Several other climbers appear almost leafless, but have a profuse growth of tough, twisting, clasping stems, which I afterwards learned, were much used by the Maoris for weaving their eel pots together, or tying fences, being very durable even when kept under water.

To the most detestable of all the climbers has been given the name of "the Lawyer,[14]" and we may not unreasonably believe that he who bestowed that name must have suffered, not the "extreme penalty of the law," but all its most cruel and torturing hindrances and damages, the accumulated misery of which, led him to name this vicious and obstructive plant after his persecutors. The lawyer is a bramble, with all the aggressive properties of his race, exaggerated and intensified. I first met with it when walking amongst some of the common brake fern, six or eight feet high, and on a sudden found my legs tied up. Knowing that ferns had not that peculiar habit, I looked and groped down to see what trap I had got into, and found myself in the grip of a thicket of lawyer. The long wiry stems close-set with strong spines, stretch in all directions for yards, scratching and tearing whatever strives to penetrate their spiteful barricade. I have seen good stout

---

[12] Rimu - *Dacrydium cupressinum*
[13] Puawhananga - *Clematis paniculata*
[14] Tātaramoa or Bush Lawyer.

moleskin frayed almost to lint in a struggle with the "lawyer." Once in making my way with a companion through a jungle where it abounded, a long spiny strand caught me over the nose and cheeks, and my friend stumbling at the same instant in another part of the tangle, drew the string of thorn smartly across my luckless visage, leaving a saw mark, which did not soon depart. The leaf of this bramble is small, and the fruit like a very little raspberry.

In this "bush" (the general term for any patch of wood or scrub,) I saw the largest kind of that poisonous family of plants known only too well by Southland settlers, as Tutu[15], (pronounced Toot.) The tree Tutu, grows to a diameter of eight inches, and is perennial; the other species are annual. The leaf is like that of the common fuchsia, the flower not showy; the fruit grows like a bunch of currants, each being a very dark purple berry, cleft deeply into quarters, with a cluster of small seeds in the central hollow. This fruit is sweet but insipid, and is frequently eaten; I have often eaten it myself, but carefully avoided the seeds, which are highly poisonous. Many cases have however, occurred, in which even the pulpy part has proved fatal. A man who had recently ate some, became perfectly mad, and violently convulsed, foaming at the mouth and grinding his teeth horribly. I am not aware what remedies were used, but he recovered. All the varieties of tutu possess the same general characteristics, although plants of different size and aspect. My readers will become more acquainted with them as my experience is further described.

---

[15] Genus *Coriaria*

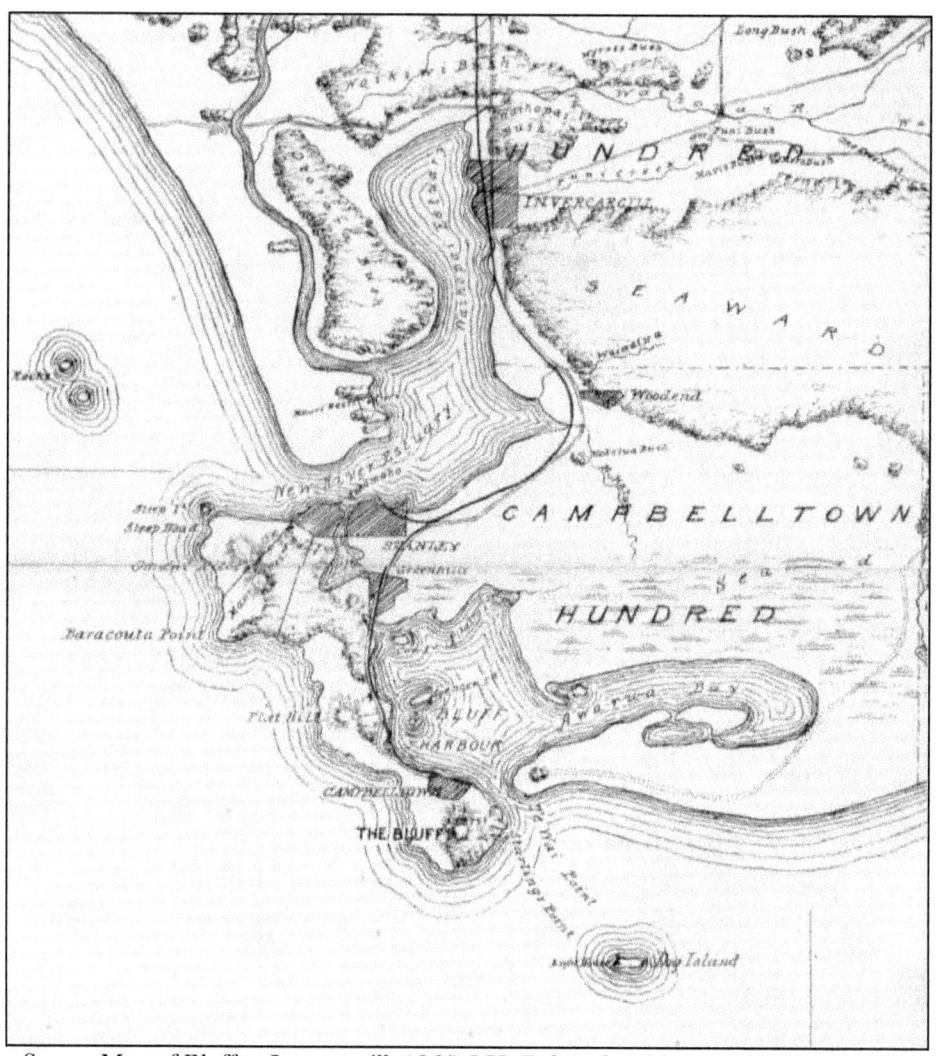

Survey Map of Bluff to Invercargill, 1865. J.H. Baker. Southland Lithographic Press.

Twenty Months in Southland 1867-69.

Chapter II

The Oreti River – Invercargill Pavement - Water Shops - The "Company" – Hotels – Wagons Eastern Road – Cockatooers - Company's Produce.

Having passed through the bush, we entered on the bogs. These are peat-bogs on which coarse high grasses and some flax grow, and cattle feed over them, but the ground is all soft and spongy, and unsafe for horses. The railway is carried along an embankment. Approaching Invercargill, we came in view of the estuary of the Oreti river (commonly called New River) and of the Waikivi[16], a smaller stream which half encircles the town. The surrounding country is a flat expanse of alternating bog and bush, and the New River is full of mud-flats, as scarcely to tell as a river in the monotonous landscape[17].

The railway station at Invercargill is large enough for ten times the traffic there is at present, or in all probability ever will be. Quitting it, we entered the town, which stands on ground slightly higher than the bog we had traversed. There are two principal streets, in one of which there are houses on both sides for about a hundred yards, and in the other, houses stand on one side only, and not continuously. With three exceptions, all the buildings are wood and iron. The Custom House is brick, so is the store of Messrs. Calder and Blacklock, and one private residence. There are Protestant and Roman Catholic Churches, and a Dissenting Chapel, all of iron and wood.

The streets are extraordinarily wide, much wider than any in Melbourne, and as the latter city may count for inhabitants by thousands, to the units of Invercargill, the disproportion is strikingly

---

[16] *Waikivi* is a southern Maori pronunciation of *Waikiwi*, Presently it refers to a creek and suburb in North Invercargill. The river the narrator is talking about is probably the Waihopai.
[17] Much of this estuary has since been reclaimed (see *A History of New River Estuary and its Environs* 1977)

evident. The foot-ways are wider also, and covered with wooden gratings, made of Tasmanian battens nailed to sleepers at each side, and leaving spaces the width of a button between each. This gridiron contrivance serves to keep the passengers out of the mud; but to catch the toe of a boot against the bars of the grating and to be laid prostrate is not a pleasant incident of travel, though a common one. The roadways are macadamized in the town, and for five miles out in an easterly direction. Formerly wagons and drays were continually seen stuck fast in the streets.

Water Works are unnecessary to the residents of Invercargill. Every householder digs a well of six feet deep, and is provided for ever.

There are still some good shops, although the trade of most has greatly fallen off since the "Company" discharged so many workmen and generally retrenched its expenditure. This company, so important to Invercargill, was formed in Scotland, (where most of the shares were taken up) for the purpose of clearing land of the native flax and tussocks, and replacing this growth with English grasses, for feeding stock. Hundreds of labourers were employed, numbers of steam-ploughs purchased, the flax cut up and burned, and the grass seed sown, but finding soil, or climate, or both, uncongenial, the grass either would not grow at all, or grew so thin and spindly, as to be useless. Returns wholly inadequate resulting from the enormous outlay made on the various large stations bought by the company, the labourers have been discharged, all but a few, and the concern threatens a total collapse. The company's management has been, none of the thriftiest in some instances. A fine crop of turnips, fed off by sheep about a third part, was never pulled, but two thirds left in the ground, and finally ploughed in again.

Only about half the tenements in the town are occupied, and the number of empty dreary-looking houses and huts, give the place a most desolate aspect[18]. No gardens encompass these which have residents, nor does any effort appear to be made to adorn or beautify them. There are three good hotels, the Southland Club, the Prince of Wales, and the Princess. The theatre is opened at long intervals, for short seasons. The Hospital has but very limited accommodation for poor patients. There is also a Lunatic Asylum. Medical practitioners are scarce in the colony, the population being too scattered to afford them support.

I only remember two manufactures here, a ropewalk, where the native flax is used, and Martin's brewery, where excellent beer is made. A jetty was built at Invercargill Heads, at a cost of some £30,000, but no vessels go alongside, or over have gone, for before its completion, the tide of traffic turned in favour of the Bluff, as the New River has a bar at the entrance, and is now so completely deserted, that even the pilot is removed[19].

Bullock waggons here are drawn by ten, twelve or fourteen oxen, usually twelve, and horse waggons by six or seven horses. Every vehicle has a tilt over it, and every man wears or carries an oilskin or mackintosh, heavy rains being frequent and unexpected.

I procured a good horse for my onward journey, and was fortunate in meeting with an old resident who was travelling in the same direction as myself; companionship on a road where passengers are scarce being an advantage to both of us; and one wretched rainy morning in the beginning of October, we made an early start on the eastern road from Invercargill. Looking round in any direction, swamp and patches of bush composed the view; a flat, desolate and dreary scene, with neither mountain nor hill visible. Coming very soon to the end of the scrap of macadamized road, we plunged into the universal mud which spreads beyond, and our horses floundered

---

[18] The West Coast gold rush between 1864-67 had enticed many prospectors away from Invercargill.
[19] The jetty was sited at Mokomoko Inlet and was serviced by the township of Stanley.

through it as best they might, till we reached the Bridge Inn[20], which derives its name from the adjacent bridge over a small stream. The house is a good two-story wooden building, kept by a Tasmanian. Many small settlers possessing from 40 to 500 acres of land each, dwell in this neighbourhood, and are turned "cockatooers[21]." Their cottages are built of native timber, and even the chimneys are mostly wood, no stone for masonry existing near; sometimes the shingle stones are used. Fences are made of posts and rails, sod walls, or wire. Oats and barley are grown, pigs fed, and some dairying carried on. In the gardens the small English fruits succeed, but the continual winds are destructive to the larger kinds. The farm produce finds a market at Invercargill.

The road here being confined between either fences or ditches, the sea of stiff black mud of which it consists, and which is nearly three foot deep, was our only track, and an involuntary growl the only response to the grunts of our poor struggling horses, as they laboured and wallowed through it for ten weary miles. My faithful dog, with his long silky coat clotted in masses by the tenacious mire, often stuck fast for a while, till by desperate efforts he extricated himself and plodded on. We either traversed or skirted several of the company's stations, for 15 or 16 miles in this neighbourhood; one is called Morton Mains, of others the names have escaped my memory. The land was originally purchased from the Government at £1 per acre, and a large expenditure has been going on in improvements for years past. The houses, men's huts, and farm buildings all appear very good; and the fencing is good also; most commonly formed of posts and top-rail of timber, with wire below. I counted 33 slacks of oats in one paddock, some seven months after harvest. The land when cleared is cropped before the grass is laid down. The company supply some excellent beef to the Invercargill market, but I was told that their shop did not answer so well, that fluke[22] was amongst them, and foot-rot prevalent. Pigs and bacon are also among the company's staple commodities.

---

[20] Situated on East Rd on the outskirts of modern Invercargill. The name 'Bridge Inn' is retained in a road near Roslyn Bush.
[21] Historic Australian slang for Tasmanians
[22] A disease of the liver

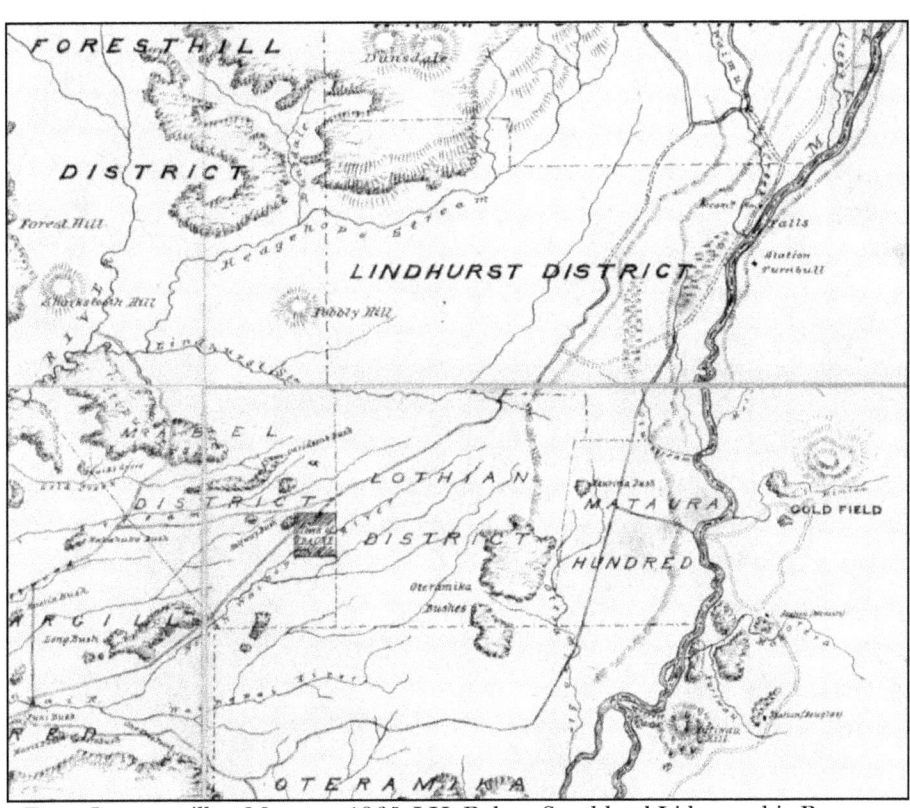
From Invercargill to Mataura, 1865. J.H. Baker. Southland Lithographic Press.

Twenty Months in Southland 1867-69.

Chapter III

The Mataura - Dangerous Fords - Suspension Bridge
Lampreys – Hokanui - Tutu
"Blue-bottle Flies" – Waimea - " Wild Irishman"
"Paradise Duck" - "Another Providence"
Switzers - Tapanui - Lignite.

Emerging at last from the fenced mud-way at Dacre, or Halfway bush, we found another "Accommodation house" (as country inns are called here), kept by the Howell brothers, from Geelong[23], and I can heartily commend it as affording comfortable quarters for man or beast. The license fee for such houses is £10 a year. From hence, looking across the valley of the Mataura, some low hills afford some relief to the eye, weary of the monotonous, bare, level land which still forms the foreground and middle distance of the view.

Beyond Dacre we passed over a few miles of very poor flat country, with a scattered growth of flax and coarse tussocks, but no sign of any kind of habitation was visible; then crossing some slightly higher ground, we came upon an extent of flat country running parallel with the Mataura. This river flows from the snowy ranges, and varies in width from about 30 to 60 yards, running at the rate of six miles an hour in a winding course which is constantly changing, the rapid stream cutting into the gravelly banks, first on one side, then the other, wearing them into abrupt cliffs, whilst long sloping points form opposite each precipitous bend. The fording places are thus never to be depended on, the sloping points making easy entrances but the opposite walls of gravel very awkward exits for the traveller. On one occasion, sometime after this exploratory visit, I had a mob of horses to cross here, and driving them in off a sloping spit they managed to scramble out and claw their way up the opposite bank, all but a foal, which could not get out there, and was in danger of drowning. Getting my own horse over by swimming and wading, I managed to steer the foal to a spot where he succeeded in landing,

---

[23] Geelong, Victoria, Australia.

but where my horse could not, so coasting down to a more practicable point we too at length lauded, a consummation desirable enough, water at ice temperature, or nearly, not being particularly pleasant to disport in, in such a climate.

Proceeding for another five or six miles we arrived at the Falls, where the river pours in one grand volume over a perpendicular rock, and then flows through a deep gorge about forty yards wide, which a suspension bridge spans from cliff to cliff. I was told that at one season of the year lamprey eels are caught in vast numbers; they hang on to the rocks near the Falls in masses, like swarms of bees, sometimes as large as a hogshead. At the accommodation house near the Falls (which is no equal in point of comfort to the one last named) we stayed the night; but it was long ere I lost the roar of the cascade in sleep.

Eastward over the bridge is the road to Dunedin, and from it, looking over intermediate low lands, the Hokanui[24] range of hills is seen. Continuing on the west side of the river we arrived at the Longford, formerly a police station; the "accommodation house" is simply a hovel. Here is a ferry-boat for crossing passengers but not their horses. These they must tow after them. The Hokanui station, about three miles off, is pleasantly situated on the slope of a hill, at a very pretty "bush," and the grass in the vicinity is better than usual. The clearly defined outline of all the "bushes," or patches of wood, is a singular feature in the landscape. Whatever form the bush may assume, the edge is as distinct as though it were an artificial plantation, kept with the strictest care within a certain boundary, or as if the adjacent land had been cleared up to the sharply cut border of the bush. Homesteads are always, if possible, placed near to one of these wooded oases, and hence the frequent use of the term "bush" in names of places.

In this part the most poisonous kind of Tutu is only too abundant. It is a creeping plant, running amongst the grass, and thus very liable to be picked up by sheep or cattle; the leaf is similar in form to that

---

[24] (sic) Hokonui

of the larger species. I once saw here, within a distance of nine miles, above a dozen out of a mob of valuable imported cattle newly arrived lying dead from Tutu, in sight of the road. The rapidity with which the poison does its fatal work, renders it a terrible enemy to the owner of stock, and the plague is no merely temporary annoyance, as there cannot be even a remote probability of the plants being eradicated.

In the absence of all beasts of prey to consume carcasses of dead animals, the extraordinary numbers and activity of the blow-flies scorn ordained to supply their places in great measure, and the celerity with which the bodies disappear is sometimes marvellous. The excessive moisture everywhere also assists in the rapid decomposition, the mass rotting and dissolving, instead of partially drying up, as in warmer climates and when occasional heat favours the operations of the flies as well, the return to dust is speedily effected. The fly is not the brown buzz fly of Australia, but a bright blue; I believe the veritable blue-bottle-fly of Britain.

Since leaving the "Halfway Bush," we had traversed an almost level tract, destitute of all wood or shrubs, and only diversified by rivulets and bogs, the latter lying in little basin-like hollows, and distinguishable by the greener hue of their coarse grass. Gradually vast ranges of snowy mountains became visible before us in the north; (their peaks continue white for nine months out of the twelve), and the road skirting round the foot of the Hokanui hills commanded more varied and pleasing scenery than the usual dreary spread of flat land.

Near the junction of the Waimea River with the Mataura, a settler named McIvor has a small farm, producing corn, milk and vegetables, and also keeps an accommodation house which we found clean and comfortable, and were, according to our general luck, the sole guests at the time of our visit. Were the licence fee for such houses larger, they could not be kept open, and travellers in this thinly peopled region would be deprived of their very needful asylum. Other colonies would do wisely to adopt a similar course respecting small inns in out-of-the-way nooks, where travellers have "urgent need" for rest and refreshment, but where the small number passing utterly precludes the payment of a heavy licence duty.

Here and there on the plains near the rivers are small patches of manuka and too-mattagoree, or "wild Irishman."[25] This shrub is a perfect *chevaux de frise*[26] of spikes or thorns about an inch long, each having two small leaves at its base. There are other members of this formidable family, which, if viewed as in any degree symbolical, can only typify the most barbarously rude and pugnacious of the Milesian race[27]. The name we apply to some of the Tasmanian Hakeas, "porcupine tree," fits it tolerably well. Gorse is amiable and sleek in comparison. Horses fear and dislike it extremely. The large kinds grow generally along river beds, but the smaller infest the grass in many parts of the flat lands.

A few ducks, generally in single couples, are the only native creatures I saw. The Paradise duck is a very beautiful bird, the breast a soft mottled grey, the wings clear black and white like a magpie, the neck a shining chestnut brown, and the head of the duck white, of the drake black. They are easily tamed when young, and are very poor shooting when wild; I should think the "sport" of shooting in a barnyard about the same. Nor are they worth powder and shot for culinary purposes, being both tough and tasteless. We once found the nest of one of these ducks in a hollow tree. We had observed the pair for several days, and always lost sight of the duck at one spot. Carefully searching about, we saw her track along the sloping trunk of a birch tree, which had nearly become up-rooted from the river bank, and leaned over the stream. At seven or eight feet from the ground a branch had been broken, and there was a hole, down which the duck went to her nest, placed about two feet above the bank.

Crossing the Mataura, we entered Otago; performing easily enough what, as described by a queer fellow I once met with, seemed a

---

[25] Matagouri/matakoura
[26] Spike covered defences or obstacles
[27] The original settlers of Ireland

mysterious process. He said he was "*going into another providence.*" So, being in the province of Otago, our first halt was at the "Pyramid[28];" and why that name I should be applied to a place where no shape resembling a pyramid is visible I leave others to determine. The accommodation house with its small garden stands on the bank of the river, which is here about 40 yards wide, one shore consisting of low ferny hills, the other of level ground. My way lay along the old road, or rather track, to Dunedin. This was formerly much frequented by teams travelling between Dunedin and Lake Wakatip, but is now little used. The adjacent country is dreary and monotonous; chiefly bare hills, with sheep stations every fifteen or twenty miles.

About twenty miles north of the Pyramid on the Waikaka are the gold diggings known as "Switzers.[29]" At one time some 600 men worked there; but the best ground is now exhausted, and about 150 only remain. The method pursued is chiefly ground sluicing; the whole being surface work. Some men earn £2 a week, some, more rarely, £20. The settlement is I believe under the Nokomai Warden, not being large enough to deserve one of its own.

A little to the north of the ford by which we crossed the Waikaka, is a small digging settlement. A company was formed for the purpose of bringing the water for gold washing, some 5 or 6 miles. At the present time there may be 30 men there, just making wages. In this neighbourhood I first observed groups of cabbage-trees. Continuing on the same track and traversing some low hills, we came down into a flat, on the opposite side of which rises the Tapanui range, about one thousand feet high, the sides very sleep and abrupt, with bare rounded summits. The lower portion of the mountains, and also much of the flat, are covered with bush, amongst which are some fine large trees and good timber. The river Pomahaka (or Pomahawk) winds through the valley. Some valuable seams of lignite

---

[28] Pyramid is the name of a former railway siding settlement on the Waimea Plains railway about 4km east of Riversdale.
[29] Now known as the settlement of Waikaia. Gold was first discovered here in 1862 and Switzers quickly became a bustling goldmining town with 2000 inhabitants in the area and one pub "for every three or four houses".

have been found on this river, varying from an inch to some feet in thickness, and lying so near the surface that a very good one was struck in sinking a post-hole. It resembles a clayey kind of coal, and as it burns well is valuable where wood is scarce. Some seams are very resinous and bright, like best coal, and bum with great brilliancy. A bed of lignite which had caught fire remained burning for some time, and may probably be burning still[30].

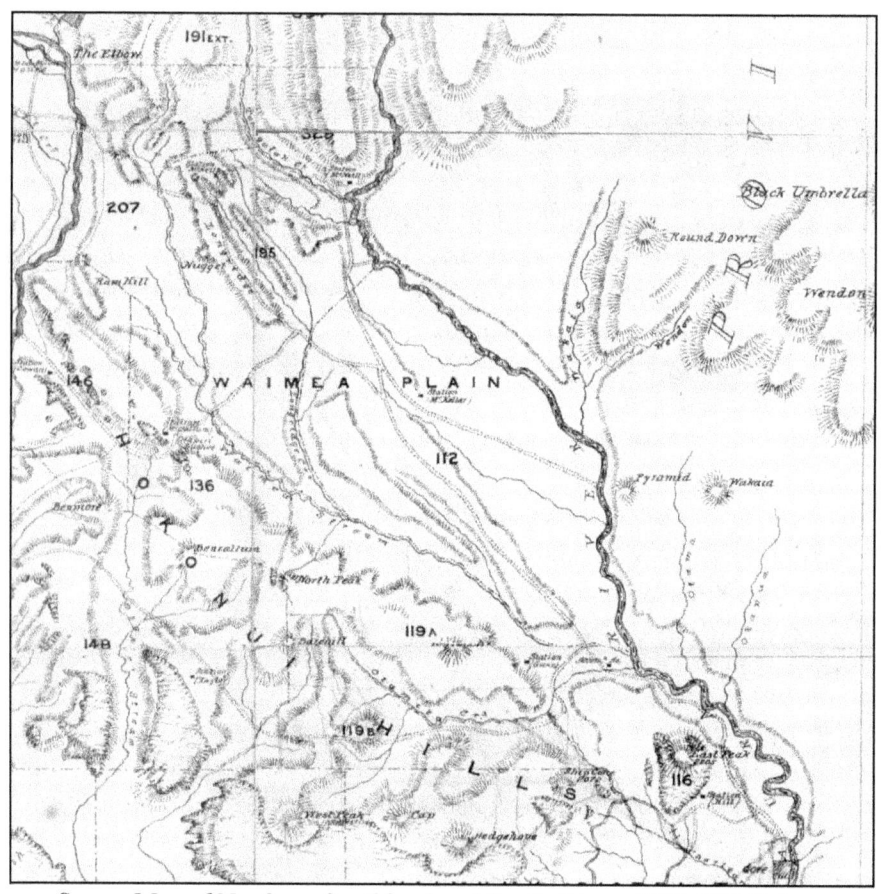

Survey Map of Northern Southland and South Otago, 1865. J.H. Baker.
Southland Lithographic Press.

---

[30] Known as the Burning Plains. The Maori name for this location is reputedly *Te Ahiaue – Ahi* (fire), *aue* (alas).

Twenty Months in Southland 1867-69.

CHAPTER IV

Saw Mills of Tapanui – Billiards
Fatality of Tutu - Mr. Pinkerton's Station – Waimea
Long Ridge - Grand View.

Having business to transact at the saw mills of Tapanui I rode up the valley thither and took up my quarters at one of the two "accommodation" houses, which is kept by an American, with a Tasmanian wife, who was eager for news of the older colonies. Here I found, in the only tolerably sized room of the small establishment, a first-class billiard table, which me-thought must have felt curiously out of place in its rough home and with such novel surroundings[31].

NOBLE'S HOTEL, TAPANUI.

N. M'MILLAN - - Proprietor.

GOOD ACCOMMODATION FOR TRAVELLERS.
A first-class Billiard Room, containing one of Alcock's Tables, is attached to the premises. First-class stabling, with an experienced Groom in attendance.
Excellent Paddock Accommodation.

COMMERCIAL HOTEL, TAPANUI.

ANDREW ALLAN - Proprietor.

This Hotel sustains its reputation for comfort and attention, and is replete with every accommodation, and specially recommends itself to travellers and others visiting Tapanui.

A Billiard Room, fitted with an excellent Bagatelle Table, has recently been added to the Hotel.

Something too, of "go-ahead" enterprise was evidenced in the bald speculation of conveying so cumbrous and costly a fabric over such roadless wilds, a distance of 80 miles. Judging however by the number of customers at the house, the attraction was "paying". The men employed at the sawmills, and in carting timber, form the population here, and in an evening patronise the billiard-table and the bar conjointly. Some of the men played tolerably well, and some were very drunk.

---

[31] See advertisement above. Both hotels in Tapanui had first-class tables. *Tuapeka Times* 1972.

My bed-room, of 6 feet square, being off the billiard-room, and thin wooden partitions being by no means impervious to sound, I possessed more opportunity than I enjoyed of hearing the very hilarious proceedings of the company until three in the morning. They drank, talked, laughed, sang, swore and quarrelled in turn, play going merrily on the whole time, and every stroke seeming as if made into my ears. However, even saw-millers' billiards have an end, and at last I slept.

Next day I visited the mills. One, the old original concern, lies some 300 yards in the bush, and consists of little better than a shed, with straight and circular saws, driven by a rudely constructed over-shot water wheel. The logs are brought down by teams of oxen; and tracks have to be cut through scrub and entangled vines, for each to be got out. The steam-mill is of more recent establishment, and the rival ship between the two runs high. Keen is the scent after a good order, and great the exultation of the successful competitor.

The timber-carters who convoy the sawn stuff to its various destinations, sometimes 50 and 150 miles distant, work on their own account, and own the teams they drive. In October, when I was at Tapanui, there were 18 of these bullocks lying dead from Tutu, close round the place, worth, when living, £20 each. This sad mortality and loss is in some degree the fault of the men. They make a long stage the last day, so as to reach home at night; the poor cattle arrive more hungry than usual, and Tutu taken on an empty stomach is almost certainly fatal.

The homestead of Mr. Pinkerton's sheep station is within three miles of Tapanui, and delighted me by its comfort and beauty. The splendid gardens and orchards are well sheltered by a bush, and by well-grown thorn hedges. The true kindly hospitality which settlers in Southland proffer to all strangers of gentlemanly or respectable character is an attribute which many a wanderer, as well as myself, will remember with grateful pleasure; and to make the allusion here, in mentioning Mr. Pinkerton's name, seems only a natural result of having visited his fireside.

On the Waimea plains, seven miles from the Pyramid, is the home station of the large property owned by Mr. G. M. Bell[32]. It comprises the only really good house, and the best and most substantial improvements I saw in all Southland. The great woolshed for twenty shearers is built of timber from the Tapanui saw mills, 40 miles off, and few masters on other stations are as well housed as the shearers are on this, in a good stone building. I have mentioned the great scarcity of stone in Southland; I never saw enough to make a chimney elsewhere. On this Waimea station is the only quarry I know. A cliff of sandstone rising from the bank of a small brook furnishes a good building material. It is softish when first cut, but hardens after exposure, still absorbing so much wet that it requires to be painted over. I believe it to be the same as the Oamaru stone, north of Dunedin, which is so much used and spoken of in that neighbourhood. Mr. Bell has a first-rate hot-water sheep wash among his improvements. At the time I was there, there were about 30,000 sheep, managed by an overseer and three shepherds, but that number has been since increased - the proprietor expecting the run to carry 60,000. The large new gardens here have formidable antagonists to success in the prevalent violent winds, which, sweeping uninterruptedly over so many miles of open plain, are most destructive to fruit trees of all kinds.

Intending to reach the Oreti River, I traversed a range of low sloping hills west of Waimea station, forming excellent sheep country, superior in my opinion to any of the plains. Sheep do better on it and are healthier, different animals from these on the lowlands. Perhaps the exercise invigorates them, but be the cause what it may, I noticed that the hill sheep were usually as active as deer and as strong as donkeys. The track here ascends a long mountain spur, grassy, but entirely bare of wood; the level country is too swampy and boggy to travel on. Near the brow of the ascent in a small gully is

---

[32] Photograph of Bell from *Otago Witness*, 31 March 1898. Bell had only just purchased the property in 1867.

the homestead of Long-ridge station, Mr. McKellar's, supposed to occupy some of the best country in Southland[33].

From the summit of the ridge, a view both grand and extensive may be enjoyed on a clear day, but a haze very frequently veils it in a most tantalizing manner. To the eastward the eye has a range of about fifty miles over the great Waimea plains, and to the westward over perhaps sixty miles across the New River Plains, and these of the Five Rivers, with the Takitimu range beyond, backed by the peaks of the great Western Mountains crowned with everlasting snow, and looking blue whenever the white robe leaves them uncovered. I never saw the rosy tint on these snowy mountains, which travellers in Europe describe us so beautiful in the Alps.

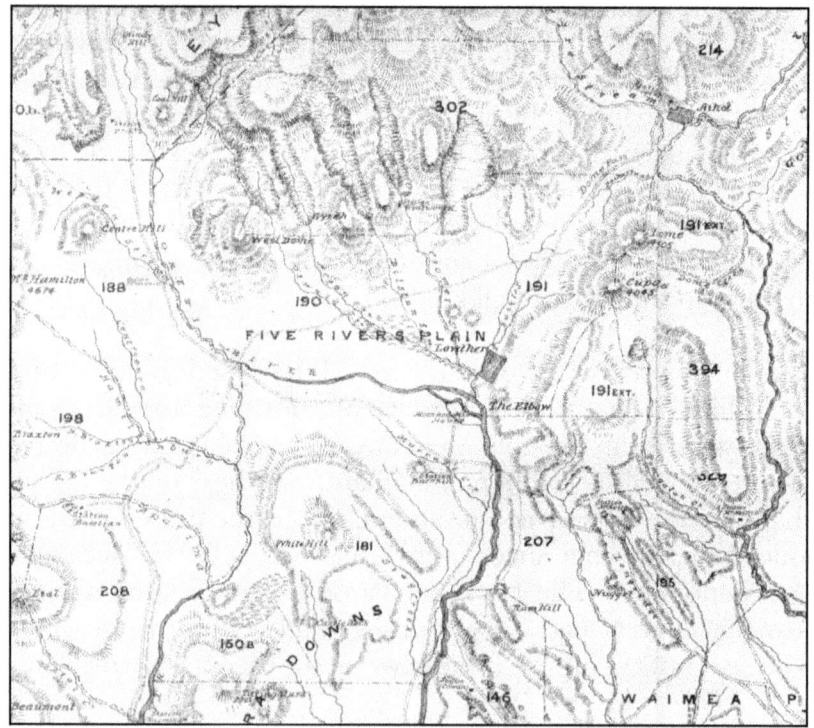

Survey Map of Lumsden to Aparima, 1865. J.H. Baker. Southland Lithographic Press.

---

[33] The settlement of Balfour was established on part of the extensive Longridge Station in the 1880's. The settlement of Longridge itself was located immediately south of Kingston Crossing.

CHAPTER V

The Elbow - "Devil's Staircase" - Lake Wakatip Gold-diggings New River Flat -"Billy-goat Park" - Moonlight Range – Family Bog - Mr. Basstian's Station - The Aparima – Longwood Range

Quitting Mr. McKellar's home station and descending the ridge (still keeping the Dunedin and Wakatip track), we lose sight of Waimea Plains, and pass for about seven miles over a low, treeless, flaxy country, only diversified by little rises and rivulets. Cattle or sheep, and but few of these, are the only animals here, and not any birds, except a few very small ones.

We next reach the Oreti River, the most dangerous of any here, from the uncertainty and perpetual alteration of its fords. It runs very rapidly between banks of shingle, and any heavy fresh causes great changes in its depth. One day you may cross a certain ford easily and safely, and on the next the same spot will be totally impassable. Fatal accidents from this cause are only too frequent.

Down to this point, the Oreti has pursued an easterly course from its source in the Snowy Mountains[34], but it now snakes a sharp turn, and runs about south. The triangle of land thus bounded is named the Elbow[35]. Here, about half a mile from the ford, is an accommodation house, kept by Mr. Fletcher. All these houses are pretty much alike in several points; the good sense of a landlord, or the neat housewifery of his wife, sometimes renders one here or there superior in comfort and cleanliness, but all have the bar, the eating-room, a couple of little bedrooms, a kitchen and a stable. A general assortment of such goods as labouring men usually require is stowed away wherever room can be found. Boots and hats dangle overhead from the bar ceiling, blue shirts, moleskin trousers,

---

[34] Eyre Mountains
[35] Lumsden

common knives and tobacco are produced as called for from divers mysterious nooks and shelves, and the celebrated Yankee nostrum "Pain-killer"[36] may nearly always be procured, being a highly popular remedy for the aches and miseries prevalent in this wet cold region. A "nip" of a teaspoonful is sometimes taken in a cup of tea by way of an inward comforter.

At the Elbow the several roads from Dunedin, Riverton and Invercargill, unite, one track continuing to Kingston, on Lake Wakatip. Goods on arrival there were formerly conveyed onwards in beats to various diggings along the shores of the lake, such as the Arrow, Shot Over, Nokomai, and others; now, there is a small steamer plying for this purpose. A land track exists, which horsemen occasionally travel over, and cattle have been driven on it, but I never heard of any team attempting it. On one occasion a passing mob of cattle started off in a panic, fell over a precipice, and were dashed to pieces. The track goes over "The Devil's stair-case" and through the "Lumber-box," titles sufficiently explanatory of the sort

---

[36] Quite likely an opiate based pain killer. The American made *Perry Davis' "Vegetable" Pain Killer* (above) was a common remedy for tooth ache and other health complaints in New Zealand in the 1860's

of country, to anyone familiar with colonial nomenclature. Scott's description of a like scene well suits this impractical region:

> "Rough crags and rocks confus'dly hurl'd
> The augments of an earlier world."

All the country around the lake is very hilly, and the scenery exceedingly wild and magnificent. A few sheep stations occupy the mountain sides, those of Messrs. Boyes, White, and Van Tunsellman, among others

The gold-digging at the Lake has now lost the fast and furious character it assumed at the time of the first grand "rush." The rich ground is all worked out, and the present race of diggers go on in a steady persistent way, getting their moderate crops out of the earth as systematically as farmers put theirs in; each on his claim, which now, instead of being an allowance of forty feet to a man, is perhaps half an acre. All is surface-work and sluicing, no sinking and driving. The Lake produces plenty of eels, but I never heard of any other fish from it.

Below the Elbow, about a mile down the river, is Messrs. Holmes and Barnhill's large station[37]. I heard that they have an admirable sheep-wash. After the sheep have been soaked in warm water they are passed under an archway, from all parts of which small jets of water play on them. I saw wool from this station, superior in point of "get up" to any other I know. The station has since been put up to auction, and bought in at, I believe, £47,000.

From the Elbow to Invercargill the road lies chiefly along the banks of the Oreti. That leading to Riverton passes for six or seven miles after leaving the Elbow across the New River (Oreti) flat, over part of the Castle Rock station, Mr. Barnhill's. To the south of the flat rises the Moonlight range, seven or eight hundred feet high, quite bare of timber and bush, but good sheep country. On the north side of the river is the Five-river station, consisting of a level, and mountains

---

[37] Castle Rock Station.

beyond, among which the West Dome rises to a height of two or three thousand feet. Rough as this steep mountain land is, sheep run over much of it.

The owner of a station near this, in the pride of his heart, bestowed a somewhat sounding and pretentious title on his property; but unfortunately the popular mind, not sufficiently cultivated to appreciate his taste, has wholly lost sight of the proper designation, and the station is only known to the vulgar as "Billy-goat Park."

The Moonlight range runs about E. and W. Round its western extremity the flat land continues in a southerly direction, and is known as Jacob's River flat, which I passed by skirting along some low hills to avoid the soft boggy ground of the level. At the spot where the little stream called Hamilton Burn is crossed, an accommodation house used to be kept, but the owner having other business to attend, left it, and it is now shut up, and tumbling down. The burn is named after Mount Hamilton, whence it flows.

Travelling on, bound for Mr. Basstian's station, I reached a notorious bog, of which terrible stories are rife, but a recently formed causeway spared me from encountering any perils in its transit. It is called the "Family Bog," the name having, I believe, been given during the rush to Lake Wakatip, when several drays having camped near, and all the oxen straying away, the whole party or family were detained some time. On another occasion a well known hawker[38], travelling with his waggon, was stuck fast in the bog, when he besought a bullock-driver who came up to give him a drag out with his team of ten or a dozen oxen. The driver accordingly hooked on to the waggon, but the strain was overmuch for its strength, and the forepart was pulled away from the hind, leaving that and the load still embedded in the swamp, until all was carried out piecemeal. Hundreds of like stories are told of Southland bogs; and the only wonder which a now comer entertains concerning them is how the poor patient animals succeed in drawing through them at all.

---

[38] A travelling trader

Quitting the road at the Family Bog, I turned off to the W., across the country, and crossed the Aparima (Jacob's River) to Mr. Basstian's[39] home station, which is very picturesquely placed by a recess amongst the hills, with the Takitimu mountains behind. All the surrounding scenery is very grand. Rough hills and mountains rise on all sides; their rugged slopes diversified by scattered patches of birch bush.

The bed of the Aparima is from one to three hundred yards wide, all shingle and great boulders, through which the rapid brawling shallow stream runs, perpetually changing its course, and not more than twenty or thirty yards across, except in floods, when it fills and overflows its broad pathway.

I found the mention of my name a passport to the warm hospitality of the proprietor's sons and overseer, on arriving at the station; heavy rain and their kind welcome detained me here a day. In the garden I saw a fine bed of young blue gums, a treasure which had been quite unexpected by these who sowed the seed. This had been bought in Riverton as onion seed, and the non-appearance of the savoury roots was richly compensated for by the acquisition of trees so much coveted here and so valuable as the great Tasmanian Eucalyptus.

Journeying onwards down the New River (Oreti) flat, I must note the superiority of the road over all other unmade inland ones. It is level, and without bogs, two qualities so rarely conjoined that I met with no other instance. Around is a splendid country for cattle, grass is abundant, and Tutu is not; but the land is not so well suited for sheep. Captain _____'s station is on the east bank of the river, a considerable portion of his land lying in the Moonlight range. Messrs. Howell and Stephens are settled on the western bank[40]. At Wrey's bush, a small isolated, sharply defined patch of wood on the

---

[39] Mr Christopher Basstian was born in London in 1820, moved to Tasmania when he was two where he grew up working on farms. In 1858 he and some fellow Tasmanians resolved to move to New Zealand where he purchased the station mentioned above, Dunrobin, and also Woodstock Station near Long Bush.
[40] Captain John Howell and his half brother Captain William Stevens.

flat, is Mr. James's accommodation house, where I and my horse and dog were glad to rest and dine.

Plodding still onwards I was gradually giving behind me the grand mountain ranges; and looking S.E. towards Invercargill, no high land was visible, only the wide terrace-like flats of small elevation. To the S.W. the river flat stretches away in the foreground, and in the distance rises the Longwood range, entirely distinct in character from the other hills, being wholly covered with thick bush, which continues to the west coast, with only small intervals of open country.

Continuing beside the Aparima until its junction with the Otautau, a wooden bridge carries the road over the latter towards Riverton, and another crosses it at a different point, leading to the Waiau district. A good accommodation house is here kept by Mr. Walker.

Survey Map from Aparima to Riverton, 1865. J.H. Baker. Southland Lithographic Press.

Twenty Months in Southland 1867-69.

Twenty Months in Southland 1867-69.

Chapter VI

Cross the Otautau - Mrs. McCoy - Riverton
Jacob's River - Maori Kaik - Moleskins versus Mabs
Mutton Birding – Fish - War-Dance.

Once across the Otautau, we are again in a land of cockatooers, and the road is fenced on either side for the sixteen or eighteen miles into Riverton. The scenery is pretty and pleasant. The lower spurs stretching out into the flat, from the bush-covered Longwood range, are bare of trees, and are partially cultivated by the small settlers, whose little homesteads are snugly sheltered by the bush, in the margin of which they nestle, looking down on their gardens and fields spreading over the slopes below.

Four accommodation houses occur between the Otautau and Riverton. Walkers' above named, Wilds at Mount Pleasant, and Hopcroft's at Gummie's bush, are three good ones. At Groper's bush, between Mount Pleasant and Gummie's, one is now kept by Mrs. Biddy McCoy, a person of some renown in these parts, being what is termed a "character." Into Mrs. Biddy's antecedents it were, perhaps, best not to enquire too closely. Now, she is well to do, and owns land, cattle, and other worldly goods. But Biddy scorns to waste her substance on personal decoration; her usual attire consists of a ragged petticoat, perhaps not so short as those condemned of late by Her Majesty's Lord Chamberlain[41], but exhibiting more of powerful understandings than is the wont of matrons of her years. A tattered old pea jacket does duty as a bodice, tied round her with string. A dubious something, half night-cap, half hood, covers her head, and a long clay pipe generally adorns her mouth. Biddy expects all travellers to call at her house as customers, and wee to that unlucky wight who shall fail in this observance, if ever he pass that way again! Biddy invariably pounces upon the delinquent, and in language more forcible than classic, gives him a large piece of her mind on the subject. Not desiring that her eloquence should be exercised upon me, I always paid her a visit in passing, and found

---
[41] Orlando George Charles Bridgeman, 3rd Earl of Bradford.

some woollen socks which she sold me, of her own knitting, a very comfortable investment.

Once, after being weather-bound in Riverton till I was weary, I started in the first lull of the pouring rain at midnight, and coaching Biddy's about two in the morning, found her still up, very talkative, and busy clearing away the remains of a feast. Biddy said she had had a ball, and her guests were only just gone; but the pea-coat und old skirt had apparently served for her ball toilette[42].

Crossing the Aparima by another wooden bridge, and proceeding about two miles, I entered the pretty, but straggling, little town, or more correctly, village of Riverton. It is built on the east shore of the Jacob's river estuary, a large but shallow inlet where at low tide the mud-flats are more extensive than ornamental. The place lies so low, that a high tide flows into the main street. It contains an English and a Scotch Church, a brewery, two large stores, with some smaller shops, and five inns or public houses. The whole built of wood, with chimneys of brick.

On the opposite shore is a long wooded point, with one large house, empty, and several small abodes. The estuary is a bar harbour, admitting vessels of about 100 tons, which occasionally come in to take wool and other produce to the Bluff, whence it is shipped off. The steamers do not call here, but a regular communication with Invercargill is kept up by a two-horse conveyance, a sort of American waggon, which runs, daily I think, between the two places, a distance of about twenty miles, over the best road in Southland, a fine smooth sea beach.

On the low sandspit between Riverton and the sea is the Maori Kaik or village, consisting of a few small huts, with a church and school-room. Only two or three families dwell here regularly. Others come at uncertain intervals. Solomon Partu[43], a Maori whom I knew well, officiates as Minister and school master, save when the shearing

---

[42] Evening dress
[43] Also known as Solomon Patu or Pukuwheti

time offers the irresistible temptation to make a little extra money; then Solomon leaves his own flock awhile and sojourns among these of the settlers. He told me he had considerable property in different places, and used to make journeys occasionally to collect his rents.

My readers must not now associate the name Maori with their old notions of a noble savage, marvellously tattooed, and robed in majestic drapery of fringed embroidered mats. What appearance he still presents under the milder climate of the Northern Island, I know not; but here in the cold, wet South, with keen and biting winds blowing, as tho' the cave of Aeolus[44] had let all its imprisoned demons loose to riot uncontrolled, the wise Maori, caring nothing for picturesque grace, clothes his nether man in stout moleskins, and finds comfort in blue shirts, pea coats, and wide-a-wakes[45]. His love for bright colour delights itself by neck comforters of extraordinary loudness, but in his general attire he is not different from the masses, and tattooing is gradually falling into disuse. Many of the half-castes, both male and female, are handsome and well made. The women, over their ordinary European dress, sometimes wear a fine mat, gaudily ornamented with Berlin wool, by way of a wrap or mantle, especially on horseback; and sometimes a father may be seen carrying a child in one, slung over his shoulders. All the Maories ride well; the women on side-saddles like Europeans; walking seems quite contemned; for few are so poor as not to obtain a horse, and usually I think they treat their animals well.

The Maories have three settlements of their own besides Kaik; at the Mokamoko[46], the new river heads, near Invercargill, another to the west of Riverton at Collac's Bay[47], and another yet further west, at Wakapatu. A friend of mine was one of the guests at a wedding at the Kaik, when there was great feasting, dancing, and general jollification. As a rule they do not like work, and are generally satisfied to exist on the produce of their potatoe-patch, and the fish they take and sometimes sell. Formerly they had a regular routine of

---

[44] Greek God of Winds
[45] Wide brimmed low-crowned hats.
[46] Mokomoko Inlet, Omaui.
[47] Colac Bay/Oraka

work for the year; at one time they would all go eeling, at another all go digging fern roots[48], at another go in for partighee[49] spearing and so on, till the seasons came round, and the time for each business returned. Now, the only regular expeditions they make, are going sealing and mutton-birding.

I was in Riverton in the Autumn, when a great gathering of Maories took place, previously to their starting for the West Coast on a sealing expedition. One merchant in Riverton had engaged them all for the season, giving to each his outfit, and a small sum of money in advance. The little settlement was overflowing with them. At every turn one came upon groups, in every phase, from grave sobriety to the extreme reverse.

I was in the Commercial Hotel, when an old fellow came in and asked for "*glass o' rum.*" The barmaid offered him a "nip," in a tumbler. "*Full him up*" said the man. "If I do it will be a shilling." "*Full him up-here shilling.*" And he swallowed the whole neat, presently holding his tumbler to be refilled, which it was, and as quickly emptied. Then he said thoughtfully, "*No b'lieve glass, b'lieve bottle.*" Something about him satisfied me he was not a Maori, and I said "You are a Kanaka[50]." He was delighted, was quite sure I knew his island, and became very talkative on its beauty and excellence, but between the idiomatic and spirituous difficulties which beset his speech, it was somewhat hard to understand. Some of the assembled Maories were very much tattooed, others had only the two bars on the cheek, and few young men had any marks at all.

After shearing, the Maories from this neighbourhood still make a great expedition mutton-birding. They have a permanent settlement on some small island south of Stewart's Island, where their whares (pr. warries) or huts remain, and also their gardens, where potatoes have been planted so as to be ready for them when they arrive. All go: men, women and children, some time before the bird season

---

[48] Or more correctly bracken fern rhizomes
[49] Flounder
[50] Pacific Islander

begins, so as to get their abodes in order, and all arrangements made for taking and drying the birds. They make beds of the feathers, and do not appear in any degree to partake our objection to their odour. Sometimes they catch fish for sale. The blue cod is similar to the fish known in Tasmania and elsewhere as the rock-cod, but considerably longer and very blue. The groper is a large coarse looking fish, but not bad eating. Partighee, or flounders, they take in the bay by torchlight, wading out into the water and spearing the fish on the sandy bottom.

Canons have disappeared too, as well as picturesque costumes. Many Maories serve on board whalers and other vessels, and become expert seamen. It is no uncommon thing for a Maori to ship as a common sea-man and in a singularly short time, rise over the heads of his European comrades, and become one of the chief officers of the ship. Large whaleboats, to the use of which they thus become accustomed, have wholly superseded canoes. The Maori quickly adopts what he finds to be good and useful, and seems inclined to let quietly drop out of usage the rites and habits which we are accustomed to consider the characteristics of his race. Let me not "rile" my Scottish friends, when I say that I have seen many Highlanders among the shepherd class, far more deserving to be termed savages, than the copper-coloured sons of the soil they are supposed to civilize.

The Maories of the Southern, or as it is sometimes (I think absurdly) called, the Middle Island, do not seem to trouble themselves about the Northern War[51], but are highly affronted if any one calls them Hauhaus[52], and repudiate the title with great indignation.

War dances are fast becoming obsolete, with similar relics of the old days. Only on one occasion had I an opportunity of seeing anything of the kind, when a man in the employment of _____ was induced to go through the extraordinary performance of the war

---

[51] The Taranaki Wars (1860-69)
[52] A militant branch of the Maori religious movement Pai Maririe

dance for the edification of other strangers and myself. Even then, in a room, and without any wild dress, scenery or weapons, it was frightful to witness. What it must have been when performed by a whare or two of chiefs well "got up" in their grand habiliments, and with all their wonted appropriate surroundings, is not easy to imagine. The most ferocious lovers of the "sensational" would, I think, be satisfied by the exhibition. "Bullock," (the name by which the Maori who danced for us was usually known), had only common European dress, and a poker to supply the place of a tomahawk.

He began by a low monotonous chant, waving his arms, and moving about the while, at one end of a long room. Gradually, he became more animated, never for an instant pausing in the succession of hideous grimaces and contortions which grew each moment more violent, and which appeared a main feature of his proceedings. Suddenly the low chant rose to a frightful roar; then he beat his breast violently, producing spasmodic modulations, or rather jerks of sound. At intervals, he tore off different articles of his upper clothing, and brandishing the poker with vehement action, advanced up the room, sometimes stamping, and at others wriggling about on the ground on his knees, but all the time working himself up to a state of frenzy. Singling out the member of our party whose appalled countenance showed the greatest terror already, Bullock advanced to him, the poor victim backing away, till fairly hemmed in a corner, pale as ashes, trembling in every limb, and with his fascinated eyes fixed in glassy horror on the half-naked demon before him, who, with his poker darting hither and thither, came up slowly, till the two noses, one deathly white, the other like a polished copper kettle, all but touched, and the Maori's tongue, elongated to a degree I never before believed a human tongue could be, lolled out down his distorted face; his howls and grunts; his ferocious and hideous grimaces, and violent contortions, at last exhausted him, and the performance ended. After a display of this kind, which he could but rarely be induced to make, poor Bullock always "felt bad" for several days, and was unfit for anything.

Chapter VII

**Station Life - Snow - Mountain Rifts - "Spaniards"
Eel-fishing - Mosquitoes - Shearing and Shearers
Howraki - Wool-carting - "Futur" – Rats - Seagulls
Wind - Sheen smothered - Billets**

Station life in Southland is monotonous in the extreme during the main part of the year, and in the winter some of its duties are tolerably severe work. Even shepherds from the Highlands of Scotland abuse the climate right heartily. Its great uncertainty is one annoyance. A fine day can never be counted on, however auspicious may be appearances, and "new chums" from the other colonies are continually growling at being unexpectedly soaked to the skin, till they adopt the universal and indispensable companionship of waterproof coats and leggings. An old Highlander described the climate so well, that I cannot do better than quote his words:

"*It wen't be rain, and it wen't be fair, but it's just a dom'd slether.*"

During my sojourn, I was for nearly twelve months overseer on a station, acting as the *locum tenens*[53] of an absent partner, and during that time had more than sufficient experience of the country. Almost all of it is already taken up, the stations varying from 5000 to 40,000 sheep each. A run to carry the last number should not be less than 80,000 acres. It will also bear a few cattle, which do not interfere with sheep. Runs are only partially fenced, and boundary-riders are employed between different properties to keep the flocks apart.

When there is mountain land in the run the first fall of snow is the signal for bringing all sheep down into the flats. If this first fall be heavy, as often happens, and lies from two to three feet deep, we have to tread tracks through it for the sheep to travel on. They do not return to the hills till spring, as the snow remains there for the winter. On the low lands it lies for a few days only, and the frosts here, though very severe, are not continuous. Mountain travelling

---

[53] Latin for "place holder"; or in other words acting station manager.

becomes unsafe after snow and frosts set in; the narrow ridges only afford pathways about a foot wide, and man or horse slipping off these falls down precipices often of great depth; even a dog, once off the track, can- not regain it. The great rifts in many of the mountain sides here are singular. I have seen them like huge troughs, 40 to 60 yards wide and perhaps 100 yards in depth, running from summit to base of a mountain of trap-rock some 3000 or 4000 feet high. At the bottom there is always an accumulation of smallish pieces of rock, looking like a great mass of road-metal ; the edges not quite so sharp as those left by the hammer, but all angular, not worn into shingle.

In riding along the terraces or "steppes" of the lower lands, the little gullies which cross them are always found to have this same road-metal in their hollows, as if a stream of it had run down. Large portions of the Takitimu mountains are covered with the same, making the footing always hazardous, and when hidden by snow, especially so. The Takitimu country is infested by horrible plants called "Spaniards[54]", which grow somewhat like aloes, in radiating clusters of long stiff flat blades, each ending in a strong sharp spike. The tall seed-stem is also covered with spikes, and when the mountain sides are all bristling with these formidable weapons, men and horses suffer very rough usage. The poor horses' legs got cut to pieces by them.

The large rivers are usually lowest in winter during the continuance of frost. A high wind, warm as compared with the general icy temperature, contributes more than any other cause to the melting of the mountain snows, and the rapid increase of the rivers; which often puzzled me by not freezing over in such intense cold, and the solution to the difficulty must be, I think, that they run too fast for the frost to catch them.

There is a lake on the Kawarau, one of the tributaries of the Molyneux, said to be perpetually frozen over with thick ice. When the spring thaws begin, the rivers continue full for some mouths, tearing along their wide beds of boulder and shingle, like continuous

---

[54] *Aciphylla sp.*

rapids, bare of all growth, except when their course is through a patch of bush. No reeds nor rushes fringe their banks, nor water-plants mantle the surface; cold, turbulent and head-long, they hurry on from their snowy source to their ocean goal.

Eel-fishing, in summer, is the only "sport" connected with station life, and the eels are well worth the catching, which, is performed in a manner primitive enough, and I imagine, of Maori origin. Cutting a manuka stick for a rod, and twisting some flax for a line, we prepared the snare by winding some of the flax-threads (freed from the green leafy part) tightly round a piece of raw meat, something in the form of a sausage, the threads covering it pretty closely; the line being fastened to one end of this, it is flung into the water and seized by the fish, whose numerous teeth on the jaws and palate all curving inwards, are hooked into the flax threads, and the fisher-man, by heaving steadily on his line, lands the eel safely on the bank. Sometimes we made fires on the shore, where a "bush "afforded the material. The eels run from three or four pounds weight to ten or fifteen; I never saw a small one caught. They are rich and excellent.

My friend, Solomon Partu, told me a story of an enormous eel, which nearly drowned him. Solomon was somewhat vague in his estimate of its weight, but was sure he was "twenty-thirty-forty pounds." He was fishing, as he usually did, with a large hook on a short stout line, the end of which was firmly fastened round his wrist, letting the hook just reach the grasp of his hand. He was in the water, feeling about for eel-holes; and finding a very large eel in one, he drew it a little way out, thrust the hook through it, and began to pull, when the eel made a dart, and bit Solomon in the side, holding him fast, and drawing him underwater; proving, according to my Maori friend, so formidable an antagonist, that in the struggle the prey very nearly killed the sportsman.

If Victor Hugo were to write a story and lay the scene in Now Zealand, he might I weave up Solomon's adventure with some of his romance embroidery, until it rivalled in sensationalism Gilliatt's encounter with the Devil fish[55]. Knowing the really gigantic proportions of the eels in Southland the tale appears less improbable to me than it may to others.

The weather is usually too cold for mosquitoes, but they sometimes become troublesome for a short time; during one of these brief seasons some talk was going on amongst the station hands of their annoying keenness of bite, when one fellow, treating with supreme contempt the accounts of his mates, said he had been in a part of the country where every mosquito was as big as a quart pot, and made a noise like a steam-engine.

"*I know a man there,*" he continued, "*as had to carry an iron pot from the sheep yards up to the house. Well, the brutes came fizzing about Jack and buzzing, till he was frightened they would eat him up, and down he sat on the ground with the pot a top of him, covering him right over. Presently he heard a sort of a boring noise, and turned towards it; there was daylight coming; through the pot, and a mosquito's trunk, like a spike nail, feeling all about for Jack ; then another and another bored in, and as fast as they came, Jack clench'd 'em with his hammer, and when four on 'em was clench'd, he gave a shout, and they lifted the pot clean up, and flew away with it right out of sight. Now they was 'skitoes -something like!*"

Sand-flies are most tormenting little pests in many places near the sea, but do not come far inland. The Bluff is a favourite neighbourhood of them.

Shearing is the one great break in the monotony of station life; it is a busy time anywhere; but here the uncertainty of the climate adds tenfold to its usual difficulties and anxieties. When the sheep are washed in hot water, it is arranged so that the shearers keep pace with the washers, the latter having a start of three or four days for the first lot to get dry. In the frequent wet weather, washing must stop; even during the rainy time, a short lull and a high wind dries the

---

[55] Victor Hugo '*Toilers of the sea*' 1866

wool very rapidly; but a sharp look out must be kept to get the sheep under cover before they are wet again.

With cold-water washing, 3000 or 4000 are got through with and shorn as weather permits. On very few stations are there any paddocks for the washed sheep; usually they are "tailed" (or shepherded) during the day, and yarded or put into some small enclosure at night.

It was amusing to see what great swells most of the shearers appeared, on arrival. All on horseback, the style of "mount" varying according to circumstances, all attired in good comfortable clothes, frequently "pants" and boots, with paper collar and smart necktie. They are now paid 18s. a hundred; the price formerly was £1 and £1 10s. besides keep, or as it is universally called here, "tucker."

One shearing, we had three Maories and two half-castes among the shearers. Solomon Partu, whom I before mentioned as belonging to Kaik[56], was one of the former. He had with him a Bible in Maori, and on Sundays used to read it aloud to the others. Often in the shed he would strike up singing in Maori, in the usual monotonous chant, varied by sudden grunts, at, I suppose, important passages, and the others would laugh and cheer him on, saying "Well done, Solomon! Well done!" They all sang psalms in Maori, but never to our church tunes; at least, I could not recognise any. All the airs, if they may be so termed, appeared to be their own humming, droning ditties, sounding just as much like war-tunes as anything else, and such I believe the chief of them to have been.

Another Maori was named Howraki[57]. He was the most magnificent and most thorough savage in appearance I ever saw, standing about 6ft. 2in., and about 15-stone weight. His countenance was handsome, with most remarkable mobility of feature and expression, powerfully and terribly so, if angry. I have sometimes called suddenly to him in the shed, and his quick, up-turned glance had a

---

[56] The Maori village in Riverton.
[57] Hauraki

piercing keenness a startling look-you-through sort of lightning flash, which I never saw in any other face. He was often heated by work, and used to shine all over with perspiration like brightly-polished copper, I was on excellent terms with all the Maories, because they said I never sought to take any mean advantage of them, and all would render me obedience and willing service. Howraki was a good shearer, but did not always care to do his best; he was very careful too with his sheep. I had rather have Maories for sheep washers than either English or Highlanders; they are so very careful. At this sheep washing, only three sheep were drowned out of 18,000.

A third Maori-shearer was, like Solomon, a man about 50, and exceedingly difficult to understand, knowing but little English. Often has my most patient attention failed to catch his meaning when he was telling me something. Then Solomon would assist, and entangle the point at issue still more. Howraki, anxious to clear all up, and putting in his oar, drifted us further from our understanding than over, till at last I had to call up one of the half-caste boys to translate the whole into English. He was a sharp, quick, smart lad of 9 or 10, who came to us a stranger, new to every person and all the business of the station and shearing shed, but he very soon learned what to do, and went ahead of two English boys who had been at work some time. He was employed picking up wool. He was offered some grog at the sheep-wash, and made to taste it, but he did not like it at all, and in fun was called Wypero[58], which annoyed him very much - "*Me no Wypero; Wypero mean nobbler, me no like nobbler.*" One day a letter from his family came for a Maori; he read it first himself, and then it went from hand to hand among the other Maories, all seeming interested in the perusal. All could write.

The shearing lasted six weeks, which, fortunately, were unusually fine weather, and ended in the middle of February. The sheep, as shorn, are turned out on their respective runs, the ewe run and the wether run. After all are finished there is a muster for stragglers, and when put out again they are not disturbed until May, when they are mustered to wean their lambs. As soon as a load of wool is ready,

---

[58] Waipiro is a Maori term for beer, literally translates as "rotten water".

carting begins; some owners cart for themselves; others send their wool part of the distance, and engage carriers to take it on the remainder; and some employ carriers for the entire journey ; the price depending on the distance and kind of roads. Teams of from eight to twelve oxen take 14 to 20 bales of heavy wool; I have seen 46 bales on one load, but that was light wool (hot-water washed).

One curious feature on all stations is the futur[59] or store, which is raised on piles four feet or more high, and these covered with tin, to prevent rats getting in. The rats are an universal plague; they appear to be the same as the common English rat, now so much too well known in the Colonies, and no matter how remote be the spot where a man may camp, some of their kind are ready to attack his eatables as soon as his tout is pitched; and no matter where a sheep may die, there are rat-holes to be found close beside it whilst the carcase has any meat left on it. A guest whom one would less expect to see at such a banquet is the sea-gull. These are often found seventy miles inland, feeding on dead sheep; whether driven by stress of weather, or coining of their own sweet will, I cannot determine, but loan to the former theory; wind here being altogether dominant over most things at times. I am no feather-weight myself, and I have frequently dismounted from my horse, lest both should be blown together off a ridge down into the ravine below. The extraordinary fury of the blasts which rage on particular saddles and passes of the mountains, even when a comparatively quiet state of atmosphere exists elsewhere, is very remarkable, and difficult to understand.

The exceeding steepness of the gullies sometimes causes loss, by the smothering of sheep. I have known a mob started down a hill, cross the hollow safely once; then split, and a number heading back, unobserved, rush up the gully again, and falling over one another in attempting to jump, fill up the hollow, and smother altogether. Instances of this kind are by no means uncommon, and not the greatest care and foresight can always succeed in avoiding such accidents.

---

[59] Whata - storehouse

Cultivation of wheat does not answer in Southland; the cold climate will not allow it to ripen. Oats are type only kind of grain which answer well, I have alluded to gardens in a former chapter, but in the station country they are few and far between.

I ought not to omit saying a word or two as to the prospect which Southland offers to the many young men who wish employment on sheep stations. There cannot be a greater mistake than for these to entertain the pleasant belief that "good billets" are to be had for the asking, to which all manner of other good things, such as managerships and partnerships, are to follow as a natural sequence. The truth is, that experienced Australians, bred up among stock, and accustomed to sheep-farming all their lives, come here and cannot find berths; how then can "new chums," fresh from English town-life, who know little more than that a sheep has four legs and wool on its back, imagine that they shall be well paid for ignorance, when even knowledge goes a begging? It is very distressing to see the numbers now out of employ, and likely to remain so. Owners of stations are retrenching their establishments rather than increasing them, and the retrenchment will be more sweeping yet as the fall in wool and depreciation of station property become more keenly felt. For young men expecting any situations above those of shepherds and boundary-riders, there is little chance. These latter, if good at their work, got £50 a year and "tucker." Rations are not usually weighed out to them, but they kill their own mutton, and receive 50 or 100 lbs. flour, 20 lbs. sugar, and 5 or 6 lbs. of tea at a time. I believe this system will ere long change to our old plan of rations. Good hands can always get work during shearing, but that is soon over. Superior knowledge and merit generally makes its own way. I knew a gentleman - I use the word in its full sense - a gentleman who, failing such occupation as his testimonials entitled him to expect, took the place of picker-up of wool in a shearing shed, and from this, the very lowest step of the ladder, his ability and skill raised him first to be a wool-classer, and then to be manager of a station. I much fear that few of the many incapable aspirants for his later honours would have the noble good sense to make a like humble beginning unless driven to it by dire necessity. We had the son of an English baronet cooking - for the shearers, and the son of a General in the British army shepherding, besides other gentlemen in like lowly positions; thankful for any employ which should save them from starvation. It were a more welcome task to me to tell of an El Dorado of wealth, awaiting all ready adventurers, but enough of disappointment and misery have resulted from unfounded hopes; I would be sorry to increase the tale.

When the destined holder of the post I had for a time filled had arrived, I too, found my occupation gone, and could not hear of any other open to me above the grade of a shepherd. Two other gentlemen with whom I had become acquainted were in the same predicament; both, like myself, with excellent testimonials, perfectly qualified by knowledge and experience to act as station-managers, but none of us able to find a station to manage. In this strait, and desirous of leaving no path untried, where a chance of success lay, we determined to join our luck, or rather, our lack of it, and go gold-digging.

Twenty Months in Southland 1867-69.

Chapter VIII

Prospecting for Gold - First Camp - Track Cutting and Cradling Snow and Ice Flooded Out - Try Again – Wood-hens & their Antics - How We Caught and Cooked Them Swallows - Crane

After "prospecting" about for awhile[60], we found sufficient indications, in a river beach, to induce us to pitch our camp on a high bluff, or promontory, in the bend formed by which, the rapid current, there some fathoms deep, made great whirling eddies. From the bluff, about a hundred feet high, the view consisted of the usual out-spread terraces or steppes of flat land, and beyond these, hills rose in every direction. A few straggling birch trees were the only wood.

Our small outfit comprised a cotton tent 8 by 6 feet, two opossum rugs, one blanket, two "billies", pannican and tin plate each, and a moderate supply of flour, tea, sugar, and meat. Our implements were a "cradle" with its appurtenances, a pick and two shovels, and two tin dishes. Our live stock consisted of "Jack", a horse belonging to one of my companions, and my own faithful dog "Sailor."

To cut the tent poles (two forks and a pole) and pitch the tent, was the first business, then to cut bundles of fern and scrub to lay on the (always damp) ground beneath our rugs to sleep on, and to cut chunks of wood to keep our flour and sugar off it also. Then we rigged the fireplace outside, setting up two forks and a rail to sling the billy on, and piling a few stones round the back to keep some of the wind off the fire. These preliminaries settled, it was time for supper, for which we had some bread and cooked meat with us; and a pannican of hot tea was welcome enough after our journey; then lighting a candle in our tent, we had a quiet smoke, and a talk over

---

[60] Unfortunately the narrator gives away few clues to his location. Perhaps given his previous travels through Southland, he may have prospected in the Waikaia/Switzers goldfields.

our affairs, and a setting-forth of the possible wonders we were now to achieve; then, coiling on our cold scrub, went to sleep. The two outsiders, next the calico walls, of course felt the cold more than the middle sleeper, and kept up at intervals a process of rolling over and over, like window blinds, in vain efforts after warmth, thereby dragging the scanty coverings off the middle man, so as pretty accurately to equalise the degree of comfort enjoyed by each.

No inducement to late-rising being offered by the luxury of our couch, we were up long ere the stars went out, and scraping the snow away from our white hearth, lit our fire and got breakfast. I should perhaps have said, that our expedition was made in winter, the low state of the rivers at that season affording the best chance for examining their beaches for gold.

We had to cut a track of steps down to the river from our camp, as the bank was too precipitous to carry up water for use without doing so. After this was done, we set the cradle, and began work. The boulders and largest shingles were first picked off, and as all were snowed and frozen over, this was not a too warm or pleasant operation; then the wash-dirt was shovelled into the cradle; the rocking motion given to it causes the larger atoms of gold to settle against a ridge in the bottom slide of the cradle, whilst lighter matters wash away[61].  The minute scales and dust are caught in the fibres of the plush[62], with which the sides and bottom of the cradle are covered. The slide must be washed out several times a day, as the black sand, of which

---

[61] See image above.
[62] A velvet like textile used to capture the gold particles.

there is a great quantity, sets firmly on it; rocking does not disturb it, and gold cannot settle down through it. The slide is carefully washed in a dish, and the plush taken off and also washed, face downwards, to get the fine gold out of its fibres. "Panning off" we usually did at night, in the tent, as it is a long and tedious process. After washing off all the sand that will go, wet, the remainder is dried, and the sand blown off, but in doing this, light particles of gold are blown away too. Some gold is so thin and light, that if shaken in a pan of water it will float.

After we had been working here steadily for some weeks, a northerly wind caused a temporary thaw, and the melting snow raised the river suddenly two feet, flooding all the ground we were working on, and putting a stop to our labours in that locality. We next "prospected" for about a fortnight, finding gold everywhere, but in too small quantities to pay for getting it. Then the river we had been on before, became lower again in the succeeding frosts, and we found a place further down than our old Bluff, offering about the same prospect we had there, but with a less steep beach, and a larger surface exposed. Here we pitched our tent in a thick Manuka scrub, which sheltered us in some measure from the wind, but had the disadvantage of being dark, and receiving very little sunlight. Snow foil frequently, the frosts were very severe, and the mornings very cold, making our work of handling stones all over ice and snow pretty sharp. The river seemed even colder than the ice; I believe, as I said before, that if it could have stopped for a minute, it would have been hard ice, but it ran too fast to freeze. Here our cradle-work went on again as before.

A rather troublesome, but most amusing visitor in our solitude, was the native wood-hen[63], of which a large number frequented the neighbourhood. The male should naturally be called a wood cock, but he never is, nor do I know any distinctive marks denoting difference of sex. They are the size of a small common fowl, with quail-like plumage, of buff and black ; the eyes are very handsome, bright, quick, and intelligent;- and the bill large and powerful.

---

[63] Weka

At each step they make, the tail gives a spasmodic jerk upwards, conveying a droll expression of part conceit to the bird's demeanour. They cannot fly, the wings have only two joints, the last one consisting of small bones almost like fingers. The wood hen has not a breast bone, but ribs, like an animal, and the viscera more resemble those of a pig than a bird, being without crop or gizzard. The birds are omnivorous, eating anything, and everything, whether fresh or foul, meat, bread, worms, &c. Their inquisitive curiosity is equal to their appetite; they used to get into our tent and steal our soap or candle, and anything shining is very attractive to them. I knew one to carry off a bright tin pannican; and if my handkerchief fell, one would come daintily jerking up to it, with his bright eyes glancing quickly about, and seizing the prize, back off with it into the scrub, stern first. I watched a fellow one day, making acquaintance, evidently for the first time, with a raw potatoe. He came cautiously up, examined it all round, looked slyly about him, pecked at it to taste, and then with approving decision, drew himself upright on his toes, with his beak in the air, and bringing it down with a quick stroke, plunged it deeply into the potatoe, which he raised aloft, and carried off into the bush. Their note is very odd, as if made by two instruments together; a clear whistle, on about six ascending notes, dwelling awhile on each, accompanied by a whirring, buzzing sound, slightly like the drone of a bagpipe. By going into the bush and imitating this, I could at any time draw them round me. They come peeping and craning to see whence the sound comes, and are easily captured in Maori fashion, by keeping some object moving, to attract their attention, a small bird, or a bit of paper or rag, or a bunch of leaves will do, and whilst you keep this in motion, you have a stick with a running noose at the end, which you pass over tie head of the poor inquisitive bird, and end his inquiry and life at the same time.

When we caught wood hens we were very glad to cook them; and it was done in this wise:- Having plucked and singed them they are carefully scraped to remove the outer skin, which comes off, leaving the inner one white and nice; but it is thick. Making an opening in the back, we disembowel our game; then, having had a stone getting red hot the while our other proceedings have been taking place, and this stone having been selected as about the size and shape to fill the interior vacuum we have created, we carefully insert it therein, and spit the bird on the end of a stick stuck in the ground, and leaning to the fire, to roast, with the stone in his inside. I think it highly probably that in a less inclement climate, and with more variety of food, wood hen would not be deemed a delicacy; but in our cold quarters and meagre larder the fat, pork-like flavour was far from despicable. The native name for the bird is weeta[64]. My dog frequently caught wood-hens on open ground, after he grew accustomed to their cunning doubling and short turns, but a novice in the chase becomes mystified and beaten altogether.

On the West Coast a bird somewhat resembling the wood-hen, but as large as a turkey, is found, called the kiwi. Flocks of swallows, or what we took for such, frequented the river beaches, sitting on the banks of shingle by hundreds, and making a great commotion and twittering when disturbed. They were as large as swifts, slate colour, with a black patch on the head. A large and very grand looking white crane sometimes appeared, standing nearly three feet high; the most noble bird of his kind I ever saw.

---

[64] Weka

Twenty Months in Southland 1867-69.

Chapter IX

Prospecting Again - Cutting a Face
Building Dam and Hut - Blue Ducks - Hawks.

Our utmost gain being but a sorry return for our labour, we "prospected" about occasionally, and dug in many places to try for a better location; at last we found one which seemed likely to pay. It lay off the river beach, on a terrace parallel to it; and as the yield would not, we knew, pay for cradling, we had to bring the water to do part of our work for us. A mile higher up the river, a small stream joined it, which flowed down from a terrace of greater elevation than ours. By striking this stream a mile back from the river, and bringing it by means of a sluice down on our work, we should gain the water power we required. To do this it was necessary to cut a race, a mile and a half long; and we resolved to do it. Getting a new fit-out of tools, spades, picks, and shovels, we set to work, taking our levels with a spirit-level and a straight-edge. Where there was plenty of fall in the ground we cut our race as small as would suffice, and where the fall was but little we cut a broader channel. When I add that in eight days this mile-and-half of race was cut, I need not say that we were not idle.

The next thing was to put a dam across the old bed of the stream to raise the water six feet, so that it might reach the level of our race. This done, we cut a flood-race, to prevent the dam from being washed away by a larger body of water. Having thus brought the water to our claim, we opened a face in the terrace, so that we could cut our tail-race in the reef; and our ground lying near the slope of the terrace, the water we used got away without our having to dig a channel for it.

Where water is brought on to a claim in a wide level, a channel must also be dug to get rid of the water, and for it to carry the "tailings" (used wash-dirt) with it, and this is often the greatest labour of the whole. Some tail-races are a mile long, and in these which have not sufficient fall, the tailings accumulate, and must be shovelled out every one or two days. Water is the grand desideratum. A good supply of water will often make a claim pay, which without it were wholly useless.

Having carefully made our preparatory arrangements, we began again with renewed hope and vigour. Probably these details of my gold-seeking expeditions may seem trite and trifling, should they be perused by older brethren of the craft. I do not write for them, but for these like the friends who have questioned me with such eager interest as to our adventures, to whom the routine of gold-digging is totally unknown, and who, perhaps, think it as easy as to pick pebbles out of a gravel bank.

Our auxiliary, the water, coming over the face of the bluish-slate cliff, fell on the wash-dirt below, bringing with it the masses, large and small, which we loosened from the top. One person is constantly employed forking the wash-dirt to keep it in motion, and fling out the larger stones; the smaller ones and the light matter flow away, and the gold settles to the bottom.

This manner of work renders a perpetual soak to the skin inevitable. The water falling from a height makes a gigantic shower bath for a good space round, and keeps the ground beneath in one continued pool and slush, ensuring one's legs being wet to the knees from below, which, with the intense mid-winter cold, was about as pressing an invitation to rheumatism as one need give; and the evil genius we thus invoked was not slow to come amongst us. Nevertheless we got through our fifty or sixty tons (cubic yards) of stuff in a day on an average.

Believing that we should remain here some time we built ourselves a hut, by driving in a double row of stakes close together with a foot's space between the two rows, which we filled in with earth rammed hard. Our roof was our calico tent enlarged, and though as it was not rain-proof, an occasional sprinkling would sometimes arouse a sleeper, and cause him to duck nimbly under his coverings, still our new abode was greatly in advance of our former ones, and having the turf hearth and low chimney inside, so that we could dry our soaked clothes at night, we found it far more comfortable. We also built up bunks off the ground for sleeping in, and established a camp oven, in the lee of which I distinguished myself, as indeed, we all three did by turns. The thorough good temper with which my two mates, and I hope myself also, met our luck, nether good or bad, was no small item in our capabilities for endurance of our joint difficulties.

One or other of us had to go for supplies at intervals, taking Jack to bring them home, sometimes a distance of fifteen miles over a rough country, abounding with swamps and bogs. Jack was very clever in navigating through them, carrying his load quite safely, his guide being on foot beside him. He used to run out, but always kept near camp.

There were some blue ducks in the river which we found better eating then the paradise duck. Their colour is a bluish gray or slate colour all over, and they have a curious sort of sucker at the end of the bill. If a stone be flung near them in the river they dive instantly, and after some time come up again in just the same place. I fancy they must swim against the current whilst under water, and from its rapidity cannot, make way, and so come up where they went down. They make a peculiar whistling noise. One day I saw a hawk strike one flying close to the water and hold on, the duck striving to dive, and the hawk turning over and over with it in the struggle. At last the hawk, nearly drowned, loosed his hold and rose, when the duck dived out of sight, but in a little time rejoined its mate which bad been whistling for it ever since the tussle began. The hawk was similar to our Tasmanian swamp hawk, and is the only species I saw in Southland. It does not build in trees, but makes a nest on the ground amongst rushes.

Twenty Months in Southland 1867-69.

Chapter X

Gold Failing – Remove - Flooded Out again
More Removes – Building Hut - Making Dams
Kokabulla - Welsh and French - Cau-cau - Kakapo
"Charleys" - Recall

After continuing our work steadily for some weeks, we found that the gold was diminishing instead of increasing in quantity as we went on, and we decided on another remove, to another part of the river beach. Making another race, we carried our stream of water to our new claim. Here we needed a sluice-box with a false bottom, which is a plank the same size as the bottom of the box, raised a quarter of an inch above it, and bored with a number of auger-holes, under which the gold collects. This beach promised well, but unluckily, when we had been on it five days only, the river rose four feet in one night, swamping our works, and we had to wade in up to our middles, to get the boxes out. The gold found here was too fine for "panning off," and we amalgamated it instead. A man once working near us, who was not aware of the affinity of quicksilver for tin, washed his amalgam in a tin dish, and was puzzled by not seeing any of it; he washed, and looked, and washed again. All his gold and quicksilver was stuck to the tin dish.

One of my good mates having been appointed to a better berth, now left, and my remaining comrade and I, having been washed out of our beach location, went prospecting for a week to another diggings, six miles off. We packed our tent, bedding, cooking utensils, tools, and requisite "tucker" on Jack, leaving behind us the heavier matters for the present. Arriving at our destination in the evening, we had only time to pitch the tent, get supper, and sleep. During the week we shifted camp again, and prospected; and in two days more shifted to the ground we had decided to work. The task of fetching up our heavy baggage occupied us two days. Packing the sluice-boxes one inside the other, and our oven and other commodities within these, we got the whole on our shoulders, between 200 and 300lbs. weight, and carried it off. The country we had to traverse was very rough, full of gullies, creeks, and bogs, and we had to rest pretty often, but got our burden safely halfway the first day, left it, and came to our camp for the, night, returning next day, and bringing it home. We built a hut of short logs about three feet high, with our tent for roof. This abode was inferior in luxury to our stake-and-earth hut, but we had made ourselves too comfortable in that, and did not care to leave it. We made our chimney of logs also, lined with stones and clay, and had raised bed-places.

A fair amount of work lay before us ere we could begin business in earnest. Our claim was the bed of a small stream, and our first operation was to cut a new channel for the water, and turn the stream into it by putting a dam across the old one. Next we opened a tail-race on to the reef, to give a "get-away" for the stuff. Our boxes, too, required alterations, and we needed troughs or shoots for conveying the water. How to obtain these was a difficulty. Sawn timber was out of the question, being out of reach, and there were not any trees that would split into planks. We, therefore, felled six birch trees, of about 14 inches diameter each, split them down the middle, and then adzed the halves down to slabs of an inch thick; these twelve planks served to carry the water from the dam on to our sluice-box. The quantity of great boulders in the bed of the stream, rendered our work the harder, as all must be removed by hand, before we could get at the wash-dirt beneath them.

After working out our piece of thirty or forty feet, up to our first dam, we put another dam in, higher up, dug another channel and started again, and in this manner worked about one hundred feet of the creek, with very close hard labour, in about two months, with better results than formerly, but still only realizing small wages.

In turning the water from its old bed, we caught a number of the fish called Kokabulla[65]; they are six or eight inches long, and very narrow, with a bluff head and large mouth; their colour resembles the mud they frequent; they are soft and watery when cooked. Rats and mice were very mischievous amongst our provisions. Our

---

[65] Kokopu or cockabullies

mutton, a sheep at a time, hung in a tree, yet was constantly attacked. The rats must have climbed the tree, and then come down the rope by which the meat hung, to reach it, the branches had almost always large holes gnawed in them. My dog kept the tent pretty clear of the marauders.

When we took up our quarters on this ground, we were the second comers; next day more arrived, and in a short time thirty men were at work, mostly two and two. One pair became notorious for their altercations. One was a Welshman, the other a Frenchman, and both very irascible[66], each, too, adopting his native tongue when the argument grew too hot to be carried on in a foreign language; and, truly, the jabbering, guttural jargon must have given one a not inapt idea of the confusion of Babel. They were hard-working, industrious follows, and came, very hard up, with just their bedding, picks, shovels, tin dish, and food for a few days only, and nothing in the world besides. A sluice-box was essential, to enable them to do anything, but they had no means of procuring one.

We lent them a couple of tomahawks and an old plane, and they felled a birch tree, and hollowed their box out of the solid wood, twelve feet long, 8 or 9 inches wide, and six deep, inside it answered very well, except in being heavy to move about. But they squabbled and jabbered more and more, and at last resolved to part. They divided their few worldly goods into two portions, very justly and amicably, but the sluice-box remained a "difficulty". I advised them to toss up for it, and one was willing to do so but the other refused, so they adopted the decision of Solomon, and sawed the coveted treasure in two, each piece being useless, until supplemented by another length.

Two pair of diggers had built huts not very far from ours, of manuka wattled together, which is highly inflammable. Both their claims being flooded by the river's sudden rise, the four men went away prospecting, leaving all their belongings behind. Two more men, also prospecting, and living in a tent near, not finding it to their

---

[66] Easily provoked to anger

minds, came and took possession of one of the wattled huts. By some accident it caught fire, the flames spread to the adjoining one, and both were rapidly burned, together with all the bedding, clothes, stores, implements, boxes, and in short all that the four absent owners possessed in the world.

We were frequently disturbed on moonlight nights by the cau-cau[67], a kind of parrot, with brown plumage, relieved by a little red; the head is grey, and they often whistle rather sweetly, but have another cry, loud, and most discordant, like a hoarse macaw's screech. On light nights they fly about and scream for hours. They feed on flax-honey, and berries.

The Kakapo (pronounced Cookapoo) is a night bird, which I only know by hearsay, not having seen it. It was described to me as a green parrot which burrows, and lives in holes in the ground; it walks with its beak as well as its feet. Whenever white men appear it vanishes, and is now only found in the wild mountain regions.

Some very amusing little birds used to come about us whilst digging, and hunt for worms in the earth, nimbly pouncing on any we threw to them. We called them "Charleys," I really forget why; they were like grey robins, round and plump, with the same style of legs, and had away of ruffling up their small plumes, and looking angry and indignant, that was exceedingly comical. One day after lighting my pipe, I threw down a match which, falling, for a wonder, on some dry substance, kept alight, and a Charley came to examine it, hopping round, bristling up, till each particular feather stood on end, and looking as truculent and ferocious as a gentleman of his size could look, whilst he scolded the offending Lucifer. After that, we often flung a match down near the birds, and always were treated to a display of their diverting excitement. They grew quite bold and tame, coming for their dole of worms or bread.

Letters of recall, from home, reached me whilst at the last-mentioned diggings, and my companion like myself, having had

---

[67] Kaka

enough experience of a business which entailed such hard work, and returned such small profits, we bade adieu to our claim, gave our "plant" to a poor fellow who thankfully accepted it, and we came down to Invercargill to await the Melbourne steamer. The only existing relic of my digging experiment is a small packet of scale gold, now lying with other specimens, in a draw of my mother's cabinet.

Advice or comment is equally needless, after my, perhaps, too circumstantial details of our doings at the Southland diggings. I have been thus explicit, because I like faithful relations of facts myself, and think it very probable that there may be other people who may like them also.

The End

Twenty Months in Southland 1867-69.

Further reading

Visit Southland's museums and libraries to learn more about Southland's fascinating and unique history.

Esler, Lloyd. *The Southland book of records*. Invercargill: L. Esler, 2002.

Sorrell, Paul, ed. *Cyclopedia of Otago and Southland*. Dunedin: Dunedin City Council, 1999.

Sorrell, Paul, ed. *Murihiku: the Southland story*. Invercargill: Southland to 2006 book committee, 2006.

Thomson, Jane, ed. *Southern people: a dictionary of Otago Southland biography*. Dunedin: Longacre in association with the Dunedin City Council, 1998.

Online resources

PAPERS PAST – National Library of New Zealand
http://paperspast.natlib.govt.nz

TROVE – National Library of Australia
http://trove.nla.gov.au/

Te Ara – Encyclopeadia of New Zealand
http://www.teara.govt.nz/en

Southland Museums

Bluff Maritime Museum
227 Foreshore Road, Bluff

Fiordland Vintage Machinery Museum
Sandy Brown Road, Te Anau

Gore Airforce Museum
43 Maitland Street, East Gore

Gore Historical Museum
Corner Norfolk St and Hokonui Drive, Gore

Hokonui Pioneer Park
Waimea Street, Gore

Mataura & Districts Historical Society Incorporated
Clematis Cottage 68 Kana Street, Mataura

Otautau Museum
146 Main Street, Otautau

Rakiura Museum
Ayr Street, Halfmoon Bay, Stewart Island

Southland Fire Service Museum Society Inc
Cnr Jed & 215 Spey Street, Invercargill

Southland Museum and Art Gallery
108 Gala Street, Invercargill

Te Hikoi - Southern Journey
170-172 Palmerston Street, Riverton

Waikaia Museum
39 Blaydon Street, Waikaia

Waikawa Museum and Information Center
Waikawa, No 1RD, Tokanui

Wyndham and District Historical Museum
Balaclava Street, Wyndham

Wyndham Park Heritage Centre
130 Flora Road East Makarewa, R.D.6. Invercargill

www.ingramcontent.com/pod-product-compliance
Lightning Source LLC
Chambersburg PA
CBHW051707090426
42736CB00013B/2581